# The Angel Safe in You

## Messages of Love, Hope and Healing for the Bereaved

ANNIE HOPKINSON

Copyright © 2013 Annie Hopkinson.

Illustrations Copyright © Annie b.
Cover illustration: Angel with the Golden Heart.
Portrait of Robin: in loving memory of Annie's 'White Knight', her beloved llama, Robin.
Rachel's spiritual portrait: created by Annie b. for her beautiful friend, Rachel Perrin of Heart of Change.

All rights reserved. No part of this book may be used or reproduced by any means, graphic, electronic, or mechanical, including photocopying, recording, taping or by any information storage retrieval system without the written permission of the publisher except in the case of brief quotations embodied in critical articles and reviews.

Balboa Press books may be ordered through booksellers or by contacting:

Balboa Press
A Division of Hay House
1663 Liberty Drive
Bloomington, IN 47403
www.balboapress.com
1-(877) 407-4847

Because of the dynamic nature of the Internet, any web addresses or links contained in this book may have changed since publication and may no longer be valid. The views expressed in this work are solely those of the author and do not necessarily reflect the views of the publisher, and the publisher hereby disclaims any responsibility for them.

ISBN: 978-1-4525-8197-2 (sc)
ISBN: 978-1-4525-8198-9 (e)

Library of Congress Control Number: 2013917022

Printed in the United States of America.

Balboa Press rev. date: 10/30/2013

## TABLE OF CONTENTS

PREFACE AND DEDICATION ........................................................................................ 3

STARTING OVER .......................................................................................................... 7

SIGHT ........................................................................................................................... 9

TOUCH ........................................................................................................................ 15

SMELL ......................................................................................................................... 21

SOUND ....................................................................................................................... 23

TASTE ......................................................................................................................... 27

LOVE ........................................................................................................................... 29

ABOUT THE AUTHOR AND ILLUSTRATOR ................................................................. 39

# PREFACE

In *The Angel Safe in Your Heart*, I am trying to show messages of love and positive action, as if from the departed person to those left grieving. I hope we can all find comfort in the fact that you cannot truly mourn for someone unless you have loved them: love being, conceivably, the highest calling for any of us.

I seek to show the beauty in humanity, in Nature, and in relationships and families. We experience the world through our senses, so I have structured the poem around the five senses.

When death happens, we find that grief is personal, private and individual. We need to find our own path from despair to hope. And we must find a way to carry on. My sincere wish is that *The Angel Safe in Your Heart* might help some people on this, sadly inevitable, journey that I personally have travelled so many times.

In many ways, *The Angel Safe in Your Heart* has written itself… I hope it will touch a chord for many people.

# DEDICATION

*The Angel Safe in Your Heart* is dedicated to the work of the international, non-governmental charity WWF **http://www.wwf.org.uk** (formerly known as The World Wide Fund for Nature). WWF's ultimate goal is about helping people live in harmony with Nature; so my passion for conserving the human spirit is well matched by WWF's mission to conserve the wildlife and habitats that inspire my life. Thank you! To support the vital work of WWF, I intend to make donations to WWF-UK. Please go to my website at Tiger Lion Creatives **http://www.tigerlioncreatives.com** to read the Charitable Support Section where you can learn about my donations to charity.

The hare and the butterfly tree

For you

From me

Caribbean blue 3

# STARTING OVER

So here we are then - me supposedly over here,
you, apparently - still there.

But the truth is, we have not parted.
Our love is as real as the day it began.

Our time together was so treasured;
it will be again - in a strange and beautiful way.

Our love is limitless, priceless and so precious!

You are keeping me safe in your heart,
and I will look after you: nothing can part us now.

I am with you as you remember;
I have so many good memories. Thank you!

Complete

# SIGHT

When you see the moon and stars,
I am there in the inky night sky.

When you look at misty mountains,
or shimmering waterfalls, I am there.

See me in that raindrop on the petals of a rose.
I am in the gentle kindness of a smile.

Share with me all the greens of the countryside,
golden harvest riches, and all the blues of the sky and oceans.

We are together as you watch old films,
and when you look at photographs and keepsakes.

Remember how we enjoyed that holiday,
and celebrated that birthday?

Dove sparkling against thunder clouds

Trace me in that dove you see flying by or resting near you.
I am beauty incarnate.

Accept the hope I bring as I glitter against storm clouds,
like a diamond in the sunshine.

Finding a white feather is my message
of love and harmony; peace and tranquillity.

I am in loveliness all around you,
where you can find me every day.

Look for me in the gentle flutter of the gem-like butterfly,
or see me in the silken trail of the common snail.

Search for me in grains of sand,
and locate me in a mermaid's purse.

I am in caves of jewel-encrusted stalactites;
in crystal-clear streams and lakes.

Peacock

See with the daytime eye of the daisy;
and share the night watch with honeysuckle and roses.

We'll stand guard as shy rabbits and bats
come out at dusk and retire at dawn.

I am your own jewel, sparkling for you alone,
exquisite and perfect in the whole of Nature.

Watch me in the glossy sheen of the starling and peacock;
see me glisten with seashells and pebbles at the shoreline.

I flicker in sunshine like an opal rooted in rock,
always clambering to reach you.

My beauty is now in flowers, fruit and foliage;
in trees, their bark, their limbs, blossom, seeds, nuts, and berries.

Find me every day in the glory of animals, plants,
landscapes, seascapes and cloudscapes.

Strength and protection

# TOUCH

I am there when you feel the warmth of the sun on your skin.
Like you, I bathe in golden sunlight.

As you snuggle, warm and cosy by the fireside,
I share your simple pleasure.

You are wrapping my arms around you
as you put on your dressing-gown.

Find me next to you when you lie sleeping,
and let me calm you with lavender and chamomile
when sleep will not come.

I enfold you in wings of love,
soft as a feather, gentle as a whisper.

Never forget, I am your protector,
all I want is to keep you safe from harm.

Portrait of Robin

Whether you are in the heat of the desert,
or on a chilly city street, I am with you.

Feel my love in the winter snowflake
that gently brushes your face.

I am in the warm winds of of summer,
lightly kissing you in the sunshine.

We share the frantic friendship of devoted dogs,
and welcome the casual care of cats.

Feel with me the velvety shadow of a silky black rabbit,
and the tender softness of a llama or alpaca fleece.

I still hug a baby's blanket, and cuddle a soft toy.

I'm there as you splash cooling cold water at midsummer,
and soak in a winter's warm and bubbly bath.

Two angels

I feel the tenderness of your caress,
and you are cherished in mine.

I hold your hand
from sea to shining sea.

United, our love speeds us
from this earth of majesty
to the moon and beyond!

You always touched my heart,
and now I have come to rest in yours.

I am stroking you tenderly,
as the breeze gently blows your hair.

We had it all when we were arm in arm;
linked forever through our love.

As always I am lost in the wonder of you!

Love each moment as the flowers love the sun

# SMELL

Remember when you smell that old familiar scent.
Let my perfume overwhelm you with my love.

Be happy when you breathe in sweet meadow air,
and the warm saltiness of a seaside summer.

I remember the pungency of geraniums and lilies,
and the innocent fragrance of new-borns.

Fill your nostrils with the tang of the citrus grove,
and the invigorating fragrance of eucalyptus.

Inhale the smells of autumn,
the apple wood fires and roasting chestnuts.

It still pleases me to inhale brewing coffee,
and the warm aroma of baking bread.

More than any other fragrance,
I treasure the smell of you, my own dear love!

Golden ray

# SOUND

I ring out proudly from church bells,
and you can hear me in the cheeky chirp of a sparrow.

Discover me in Handel and Mozart, in rapping and reggae,
and always in our own special song.

Remember how we sang and danced to the music?
Hold tight with me now to the memory!

I am there at the dawn chorus,
and I join the birds in their sunset songs.

At bedtime I am always there in the whispered,
'Good night, God bless you, sleep tight.'

Enjoy the babble of a brook,
and the purring of a cheetah.

I am as big as thunder and as small as a sigh.

Dolphins riding a wave

Let me share games and giggles;
I love it when you have fun!

I am in the buzz of a bumbling bee,
and in the trumpet of a proclaiming elephant.

Listen to me in the crashing of the waves,
and in the mystical song of dolphins.

You can hear me in the bleat of a lamb,
and in the roar of a lion.

Freedom, equality and friendship will resonate,
echoing truth and unity across the ages.

And we will hear Heavenly music,
as we become complete and whole in Paradise.

Joined together in perfect harmony!

Picnic party

# TASTE

Don't forget me when you cook your favourite food;
I want to share a sip of delicious wine!

Discover me in the starter and the main course,
and always in your special cakes and puddings!

When spices make you sneeze, and onions make you cry,
I laugh with you, and wipe away your tears.

I will always enjoy a cup of tea with you!

You will find me in puddles of ice-cream,
in mountains of jelly, and in tubs of popcorn.

Taste with me savoury or sweet; in herbs, honey and seasonings.
I am in rosemary for remembrance, and here is rare saffron for you.

Let me share in celebration meals, and let me see you happy!

Dance with life

# LOVE

We will always have our love.

I am part of your smiles and part of your sorrow,
and I will always be there for you.

My wish is the best for you in all you do.
I am the kingmaker in your heart!

Find me and love me in the woods and in the fields,
among spring growth and in autumn colours.
I am there at the height of summer and in icy winters.

Keep my picture near your bed,
so you can find me close to comfort you.

I can feel your hurt and your sadness.
Feel safe as I am holding you, and I will not let you fall.

Sacred dragonfly 1

You are grieving, but I am still with you:
I am protected and safe in your heart always.

The pain will ease, I promise you.

Light will filter gently
through stained glass dragonfly wings,
and stream once more through open windows.

We are given challenges in life;
but we are given great opportunities too!

I want you to cherish your new life,
exploring the world without me.

You have everything to look forward to,
and nothing to fear!

I am restored to beauty, health and happiness.
There is no place here for sickness and hurt.

Happy Buddha in lotus flower

My desire is to be in good dreams, never in bad.

If you have nightmares,
let me nourish you with my love.

Please feel safe as you fall asleep,
and secure on awakening; everything is alright!

Remember with love and respect, as the elephants do.
Then move on with your life, in the way of the animals.

I am fine, I am well, and I am joyful.
My delight is infinite!

Be comforted that I have come to rest,
gently floating in a sea of serenity.

And I am happy -
oh so happy!

Rachel's spiritual portrait

I am watching over you,
and waiting for you
to join me in Paradise.

It will happen in the blink of an eternal eye!

But for now, you are needed on Earth.
Be a maverick, not a minion!

Don't give up: fulfil your purpose;
be kind, be generous
and, above all, stay positive.

There is still so much for you to do in life -
the World is crying out for help!

Soon the Love and the Light will shine around us.
I'll welcome you in Heaven when the time comes.

And we will find our place with God!

I love you always,
and our love
goes on forever.

I am the angel safe in your heart.

You are loved

# ABOUT

**Annie Hopkinson** (author) works as a secondary school and prison teacher in the United Kingdom. Previously, she was a journalist and a casting director for BBC Television, where she worked with many top UK and American actors and directors.

Annie is a contributing author to the 2012 edition of the **Gratitude Book Project**, and has also written a clear and straightforward guide for novice pet owners called **Choosing a Pet: A New Owner's Guide to the Basic Needs of Companion Animals.**

Annie lives in Kent, England, with her husband and many companion animals. More details of her work can be found through her conservation education business, Tiger Lion Creatives **http://www.tigerlioncreatives.com** and her author's website: **http://www.anniehopkinson.com**. Annie has a bachelor's degree in English Literature and a master's degree in Education. She is proud to be a Fellow of the Zoological Society of London.

**Annie b.** (illustrator) lives in Cornwall with her husband and son, and it is here she has developed her own unique style and language, in oils, watercolours and chalk pastels, creating art from the heart for wellbeing, as well as running Art from the Heart Workshops using guided meditation to help people connect to their hearts and creativity. For more details of Annie b.'s work and options to buy originals, prints and cards of images in **The Angel Safe in Your Heart,** please visit her website at **http://www.annieb-art.co.uk**.

Annie b. says: **"My aim is to create artwork that helps us all feel love and joy, see the bigger picture and the natural flow of life so that we all may dance in harmony together, be mindful of mother earth and each other, and know the Divine Oneness we truly are."**

Lightning Source UK Ltd.
Milton Keynes UK
UKIC01n2226131113
221002UK00002B/8